THE GENTLEMAN'S ALPHABET BOOK

The Gentleman's ALPHABET BOOK

By Harvey Kornberg

Limericks by Donald Hall

E. P. DUTTON & CO., INC. ◎ NEW YORK ◎ 1972

For Bobby F.

THE GENTLEMAN'S ALPHABET BOOK

PHRODISIAC

One Thursday, at tea with the Vicar,
Maud's maidenhood disappeared quicker
   Than the blink of an eye
   When he dripped Spanish Fly
In her tea, and she *prayed* him to *prick* her!

Bestiality

A juvenile bugger named Sam
Had a fondness for mutton and lamb.
    He declared, "Though I fear
    That it may mean I'm queer,
I don't care if it's ewe or it's ram."

CUNNILINGUS

This chap from the City has placed
His tongue with immoderate haste
 On the clitoral part
 Of an indifferent tart.
We suppose it a matter of taste.

DEVIATE

Uncle Bertram politely stops by
To see Margaret, and Enid, and Vi,
But induced by some gland
Or the Devil, his hand
Always creeps on to Montague's thigh.

EXHIBITIONIST

A cellist abandoned his bow
And with curtains akimbo let show
   His this and his that
   To an onlooking cat
And to neighbors who found it *de trop*.

FLAGELLATION

This Guardsman at play must assume
Black lace and the chains for costume
    While a lady assails
    His back with nine tails
And he dreams of the siege at Khartoum.

Genitalia

The things that go on in the crotch
Are anxiety-making to watch.
   The dimensions of sex,
   Concave or convex,
Drive many a watcher to Scotch.

Harlot

This husband and father, praise God,
Will continue this nice promenade,
    But if later, perhaps,
    He returns to relapse
With this Harlot, who'll blame the old sod?

INCEST

When our mother is safely asleep,
My sister insists that I creep
   Into bed where we screw
   From eleven to two.
It's domestic, familiar, and cheap.

Jaded

As she lounges 'mid carnal debris,
A Countess is bored with these three,
  Now the bearded old lover
  Leaps down from above her
To assault her again. *Quel ennui.*

KAPROLAGNIAC

This fellow likes licking one's feet,
Be one Tom, Dick, or Harry, or Pete.
   If a feminine toe
   Happened by, he says, "No,
I'm sorry, but that's not my meat."

ESBIAN

The plump-bottomed chap must enjoy
Being lewdly addressed as a boy.
   As she smokes a cigar
   In the Public Bar,
She's a Lesbian lady named Roy.

MASOCHIST

"Giddyap!" and "Gee! Haw!" and then "Whoa!"
I will go where you tell me to go.
　　Our relationship
　　Is based on the whip
And the stories of Edgar A. Poe.

NECROPHILIA

My darling is pallid and cold,
My darling will never grow old,
   And when she is rotten,
   I will have forgotten—
Another young belle will have tolled.

ONANIST

A squire commuting from Kent
Recovered the land of content
    By committing crimes
    In the London *Times*,
That his journey should not be misspent.

PANDERER

Says the Pander suggesting a tryst
To the elderly gentleman, "Hist!
   I think we can flush
    Two birds in a bush.
If you care to partake, I'll assist."

QUEER

At White's after tea at the Palace,

The Colonel remembered a phallus,

And a bit of a lark

In Regent's Park

With a waiter who called himself Alice.

R APE

In a park overlooking the city
A Rapist leaps out at a pretty
    Young lady whose cry
    Brings a tear to his eye—
But he's longer on lust than on pity.

SATYRIASIS

In the barnyard a Satyr named Jones
Is assaulting a bevy of crones.
  If this crone gets away,
  Then the pig has her day,
To assuage Jones' excess of hormones.

TRANSVESTITE

When he thinks that she sleeps, he tip-toes
To the mirror to try on her clothes.
   Then he giggles and bounces
   And shows off his flounces
And ruffles and garters and hose.

UNCHASTE

A girl named Veronica Hubbell,
Who is socially nothing but rubble,
    Has tickled the balls
    Of the Dean of St. Paul's,
In civvies, and looking for trouble.

OYEUR

Creeping out on a ledge to delight
In the sexualization of sight,
   Doctor Septimus Hare
    Fell to Russell Square,
And lost this bizarre appetite.

WHOREMONGER

Cripps worked in Bahrein, a recluse.
After years of discreet self-abuse,
    He furloughed to Soho
    And in a rococo
Bordello let everything loose.

XENOPHALLOPHOBIA

"Egad!" cried Sir Basil, "In truth,
It is wicked, immoral, uncouth,
    And a strange paradox,
    But these *frightening* cocks
Remind me of Eton, and youth."

YONI

An erudite traveller named Spurge,
With an anthropological urge,
   Climbed up on a black
   To descry in a crack
Where the East and the West converge.

ZOOPHILIA

On Sundays at noon Cousin Bea
Suspended herself from a tree.
    An admirably formed
    Stallion performed
The unspeakable act until three.

HARVEY KORNBERG was born in New York City and educated at Oberlin College, London University, and the Parsons School of Design. A free-lance commercial artist, Mr. Kornberg is now living with his wife and two children in Majorca.

DONALD HALL is a poet and author of *The Alligator Bride*: *Poems New and Selected; The Yellow Room*: *Love Poems*, and other books. He is a frequent contributor to *The New Yorker* and columnist for *The American Poetry Review*. He was graduated from Harvard College and has a B.Litt. Oxford University (Christ Church).